Master Maths at Home

Measuring

Scan the QR code to help your child's learning at home.

DK | **MATHS NO PROBLEM!**

mastermathsathome.com

How to use this book

Maths — No Problem! created **Master Maths at Home** to help children develop fluency in the subject and a rich understanding of core concepts.

Key features of the Master Maths at Home books include:

- Carefully designed lessons that provide structure but also allow flexibility in how they're used. For example, some children may want to write numbers, while others might want to trace.

- Speech bubbles containing content designed to spark diverse conversations, with many discussion points that don't have obvious 'right' or 'wrong' answers.

- Rich illustrations that will guide children to a discussion of shapes and units of measurement, allowing them to make connections to the wider world around them.

- Exercises that allow a flexible approach and can be adapted to suit any child's cognitive or functional ability.

- Clearly laid out pages that encourage children to practise a range of higher-order skills.

- A community of friendly and relatable characters who introduce each lesson and come along as your child progresses through the series.

You can see more guidance on how to use these books at **mastermathsathome.com**.

We're excited to share all the ways you can learn maths!

Maths — No Problem!
mastermathsathome.com
www.mathsnoproblem.com
hello@mathsnoproblem.com

First published in Great Britain in 2022 by
Dorling Kindersley Limited
One Embassy Gardens, 8 Viaduct Gardens, London SW11 7BW
A Penguin Random House Company

The authorised representative in the EEA is Dorling Kindersley
Verlag GmbH. Amulfstr. 124, 80636 Munich, Germany

10 9 8 7 6 5 4 3 2
003–327074–Jan/22

A CIP catalogue record for this book is available from the British Library.

ISBN: 978-0-24153-917-0
Printed and bound in the UK

For the curious
www.dk.com

This book was made with Forest Stewardship Council™ certified paper - one small step in DK's commitment to a sustainable future. For more information go to www.dk.com/our-green-pledge

MIX
Paper from responsible sources
FSC™ C018179

Acknowledgements
The publisher would like to thank the authors and consultants Andy Psarianos, Judy Hornigold, Adam Gifford and Dr Anne Hermanson.

The Castledown typeface has been used with permission from the Colophon Foundry.

Contents

Ruby   Elliott   Amira   Charles   Lulu   Sam   Oak   Holly   Ravi   Emma   Jacob   Hannah

Measuring length in metres

Starter

How is Ravi measuring the table?

Example

Ravi is using a metre stick to measure the table.

1 metre

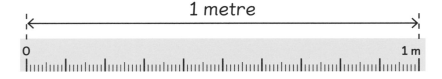

0   1 m

This is a metre stick. It is 1 metre long. The width of the table is exactly 1 m. We can measure the lengths of objects around us.

A **metre** is a unit of length. We write this as **1 m.**

This table is less than 1 m wide.

coffee table

This table is more than 1 m wide.

dining table

1   Ask an adult at home if they have a tape measure.
Look for objects at home that measure more than 1 m and less than 1 m.
Try and guess the length of each object before measuring it.

Record your results in a table.

Less than 1 m	More than 1 m

2   Ask an adult to help you measure your own height.

I am ☐ (less / more) than a metre tall.

3   How tall do you think a two-storey house is in metres?

I think a two-storey house is about ☐ m tall.

Measuring length in centimetres

Starter

What can we use to measure shorter things?

Example

We can use a ruler to measure shorter things.

This is a centimetre ruler. It is about 15 cm long.

We write cm for centimetre.

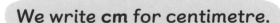
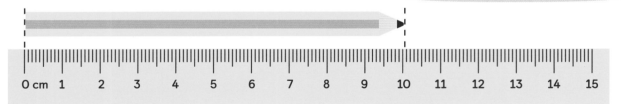

The pencil is 10 cm long.

We must line up the item with 0 cm on the ruler

The paper clip is 3 cm long.

1 Find these items in your home and use a centimetre ruler to measure them. Record your results in a table.

Item	Length in cm
spoon	
toothbrush	
crayon	
book	
mobile phone	
envelope	
hairbrush	

2 Measure the length of these items using a centimetre ruler.

(a)

?

about ⬚ cm

(b)

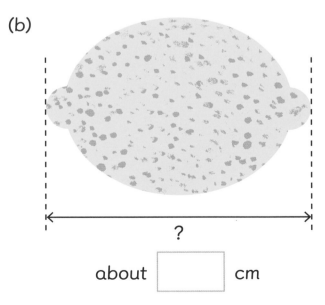

?

about ⬚ cm

Comparing lengths

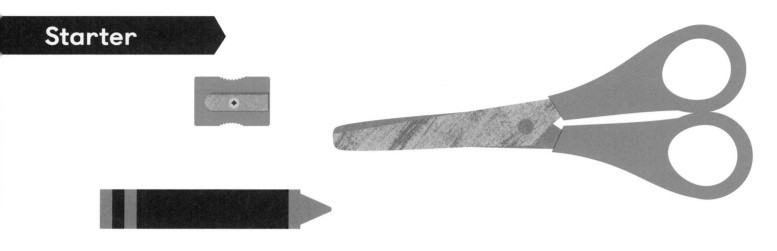

Which item is the longest?

Example

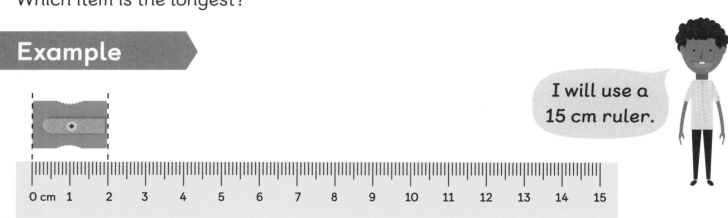

I will use a 15 cm ruler.

The pencil sharpener is 2 cm long. It is the shortest item.

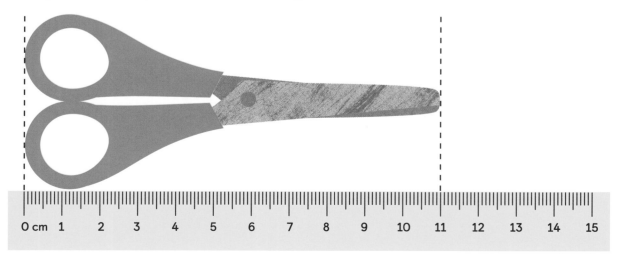

The scissors are 11 cm long. They are the longest item.

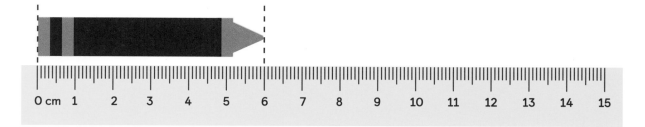

The crayon is 6 cm long. The crayon is longer than the pencil sharpener and shorter than the scissors.

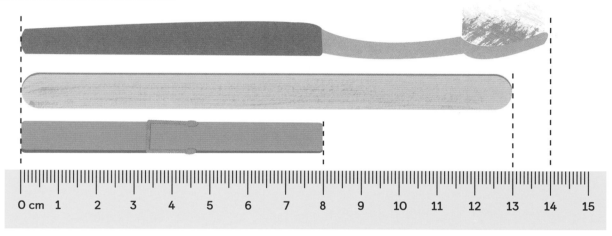

Compare the lengths and fill in the blanks.

1. The ——— is [ ] cm long.

2. The ——■— is [ ] cm long.

3. The ——→ is [ ] cm long.

4. The ——→ is [ ] cm longer than the ———.

5. The ——■— is [ ] cm shorter than the ———.

6. The [ ] is the longest.

7. The [ ] is the shortest.

Measuring mass in kilograms

Starter

How can we find out how heavy the vegetables are?

Example

We can measure mass by using a weighing scale.

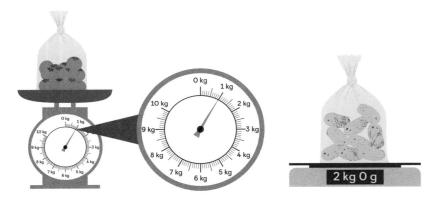

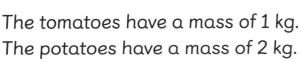

The mass of something tells us how heavy it is.

The tomatoes have a mass of 1 kg.
The potatoes have a mass of 2 kg.

We can also use balance scales and a weight to find out how heavy something is.

This is a one-kilogram mass.
A **kilogram** is a unit of mass.
We write **kg** for kilogram.

1 kg

The bag of rice balances with the 1 kg mass.
The bag of rice has a mass of 1 kg.

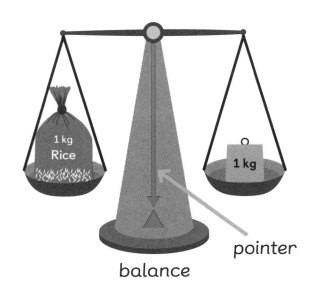

pointer

balance

10

The bag of oranges is **lighter than** 1 kg.
The mass of the bag of oranges is
less than 1 kg.

The bag of onions is **heavier** than 1 kg.
The mass of the bag of onions is
more than 1 kg.

Practice

1 Find something in your kitchen that has a mass of 1 kg,
such as a bag of flour or sugar.
Find an item that you think is heavier than this.
Find an item that you think is lighter than this.
If you have a weighing scale, find the mass of your items
to see if you are correct.

2 Find the mass of the watermelon.

The mass of the watermelon is about ⬚ kg.

3 What is the mass of each item?

(a)

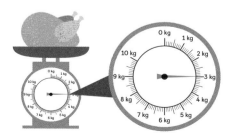

⬚ kg

(b)

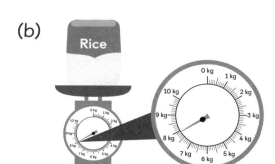

⬚ kg

Measuring mass in grams

Starter

These items are light.
How can we find the mass of these items?

Example

We can't measure these items in kilograms. We need a smaller unit of mass.

We can measure lighter objects using grams. We write **g** for gram.

These are some things that have a mass of 1 g.

The hazelnut has a mass of 3 g.

The house key has a mass of 9 g.

The credit card has a mass of 5 g.

The earphones have a mass of 13 g.

The earphones are the heaviest and the hazelnut is the lightest.

1 Look at some items in your home that are measured in grams.
List them in order from lightest to heaviest in the table.

Item	Mass in grams

These crisps weigh 48 g.

2 Find the mass of each item below.

(a) 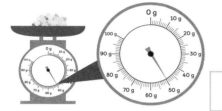 ☐ g

(b) 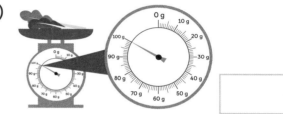 ☐ g

(c) 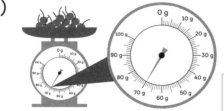 ☐ g

(d)  ☐ g

3 Find the mass of each item below.

(a)

The sandwich weighs

about ☐ g.

(b)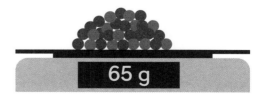

The mass of the blueberries is

about ☐ g.

Comparing masses

Starter

How can we find out which is heavier?

Example

There are 10 spaces between 100 and 200.
Each space stands for 10 g. This scale shows 120 g.

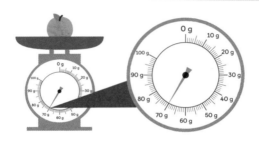 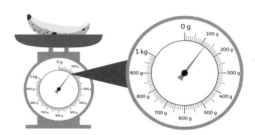 

 has a mass of 70 g.

 has a mass of 120 g.

 is heavier than .

 is lighter than .

Practice

1   Read the scales, then fill in the blanks.

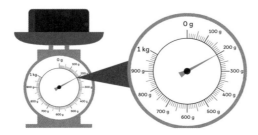 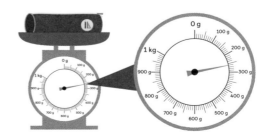

(a) The phone is [   ] than the pencil case.

(b) The mass of the phone is [   ] g.

(c) The mass of the pencil case is [   ] g.

(d) The mass of the [   ] is 60 g lighter than the mass

of the [   ] .

2 Read the scales, then fill in the blanks.

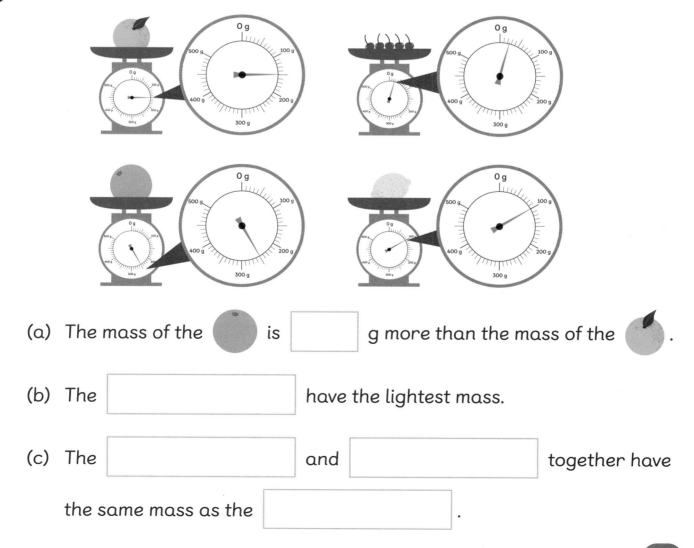

(a) The mass of the 🟠 is [   ] g more than the mass of the 🟠 .

(b) The [   ] have the lightest mass.

(c) The [   ] and [   ] together have

the same mass as the [   ] .

Temperature

Starter

How do we measure temperature?

I have a digital thermometer.

I have a glass thermometer.

Example

We use a thermometer to measure temperature.

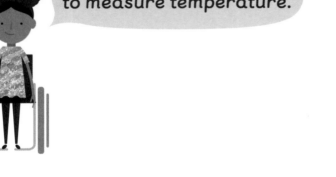

A thermometer shows us how hot or cold something is.

Temperature is measured in **degrees Celsius**.
This thermometer shows a temperature of 20 °C.
We read this as 20 degrees Celsius.

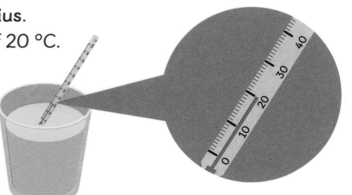

1 Ask an adult in your home if they have a thermometer.
Use the thermometer to find the temperature of everyone in your family.
Record your results in a table.

Family member	Body temperature

2 Fill in the blanks.

(a)

The temperature in the fish bowl is about ☐ °C.

(b)

The temperature of the tea is about ☐ °C.

(c)

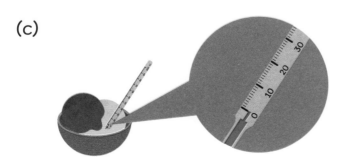

The temperature of the ice cream is about ☐ °C.

Writing and counting notes

Starter

Who has more money?

Charles

Lulu

Example

This is a **five pound note**.
We write it as **£5**.

This is a **ten pound note**.
We write it as **£10**.

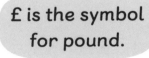 £ is the symbol for pound.

 has +  +  .

He has £25.

 has +  +  +  .

She has £20.

 I have £5 more than Lulu has.

 There are also £20 notes and £50 notes.

1 Write the amount of money shown.

(a)
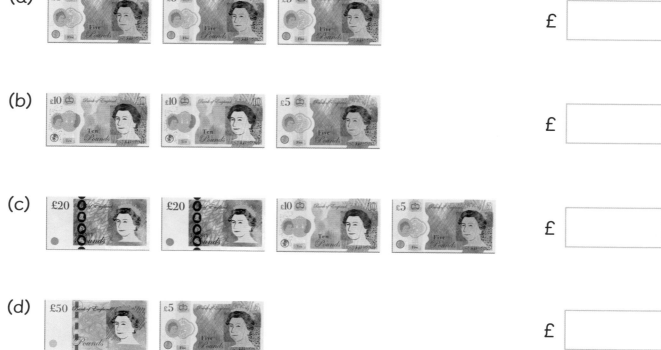

£ [ ]

(b)

£ [ ]

(c)

£ [ ]

(d)

£ [ ]

2 Who has more money?

Amira

Sam

 has £ [ ] .

has £ [ ] .

[ ] has more money.

Writing and counting coins

Starter

Does Elliott have enough money to buy the  ?

Example

These are the coins that we use in the UK.

These coins are in pence.
1p, 2p, 5p, 10p, 20p and 50p.

These coins are in pounds.
£1 and £2.

Elliott has £2 + 50p + 20p + 10p + 5p + 5p.
Elliott has £2 and 90 pence. We write this as £2.90.
The chocolate costs £3.
Elliott does not have enough money.

1 Match.

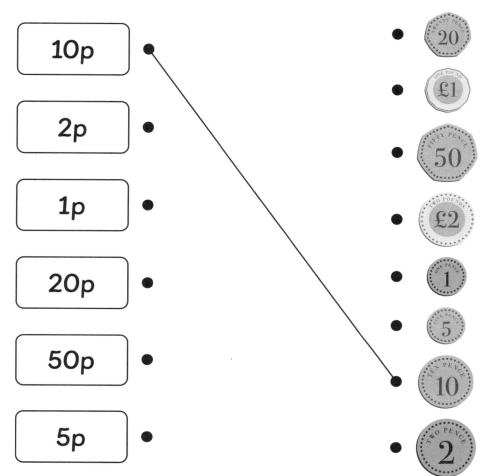

10p

2p

1p

20p

50p

5p

2 How much money is shown?

(a)

(b)

Showing equal amounts of money

Starter

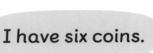
I have six coins.

Jacob

I have more money. I have seven coins.

Emma

Who has more money?

Example

1

Add the value of the coins, not the number of coins.

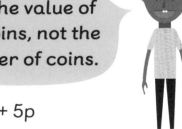
2, 3
3 pounds

50, 60, 65, 70
70 pence

Jacob has £2 + £1 + 50p + 10p + 5p + 5p
= £3 + 70p = £3.70

2

1, 2, 3
3 pounds

20, 40, 60, 70
70 pence

Emma has £1 + £1 + £1 + 20p + 20p + 20p + 10p
= £3 + 70p = £3.70

Emma is wrong. Jacob and Emma have the same amount of money.

1 Match equal amounts of money.

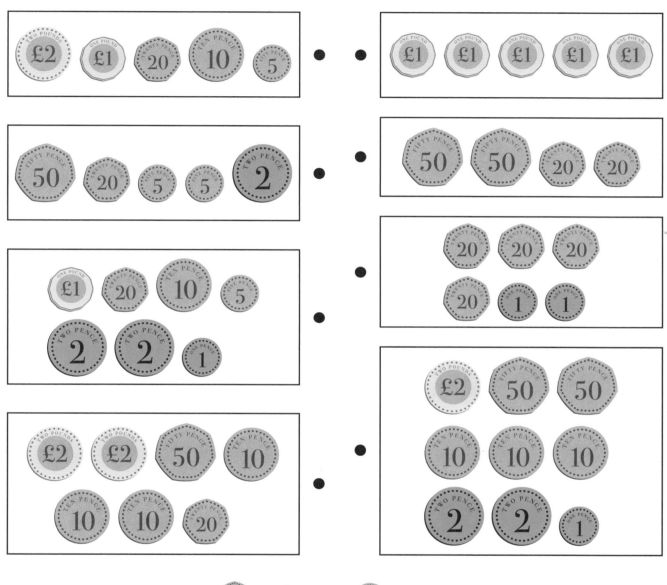

2 Can you make £1 using 50 , 20 and 10 ?

Try to find 4 different ways.

Exchanging money

Starter

Amira wants to exchange one £2 coin for different coins. What coins can she get for £2?

Example

1

Amira can exchange for 2 £1 .

2

Amira can exchange for 4 .

3

Amira can exchange for 10 .

Practice

1 Use  to show 3 different ways 👧 can exchange her £2.

2 Fill in the blanks.

(a) £2 = **4** × 50

(b) £1 = [   ] × 20

(c) £1 = [   ] × 10

(d) 50 = [   ] × 5

(e) 20 = [   ] × 5

(f) 20 = [   ] × 2

Comparing amounts of money

Starter

Which toy costs more?

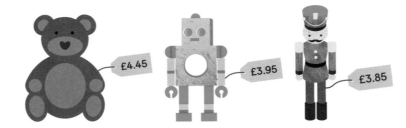

Example

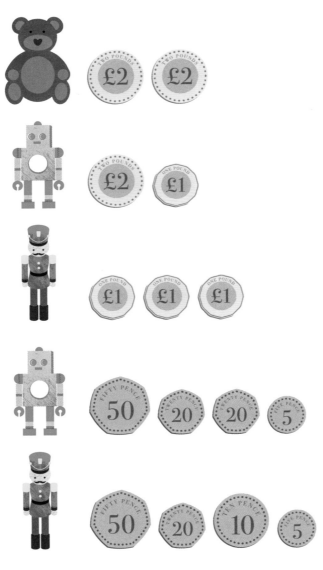

First, we compare the pounds.

£4 is more than £3. The  costs more than the and the .

Next, we compare the pence.

95p is more than 85p. The costs more than the .

 costs more than and .

26

1 Compare the two boxes and circle the one with the largest amount of money.

(a)

(b)
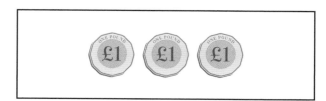

(c)

(d)

2 Compare the amounts of money and fill in the blanks.

I have £3.99.

Ruby   Amira   Sam

(a) Who has the most amount of money?

(b) Who has the least amount of money?

(c) How much more money does Amira have than Ruby?

Telling the time to 5 minutes

Starter

How many minutes have passed?

Example

The minute hand is on 12 and the hour hand is on 6. The time is 6 o'clock.

 The minute hand is always longer than the hour hand.

The minute hand is on 1. The time is now 5 minutes past 6 or 6:05.

The minute hand is on 2. The time is now 10 minutes past 6 or 6:10. 10 minutes have passed between 6:00 and 6:10.

6:20

The clock shows 20 minutes past 6 or 6:20.

6:25

 The clock shows 25 minutes past 6 or 6:25.

Practice

1 What is the time shown?

(a)

(b)

(c)

(d)

2 Write the time shown. Think about what you might be doing at that time.

(a)

in the morning

(b)

in the afternoon

(c)

in the evening

3 Show the correct time by drawing the hour and minute hands.

(a)

3:35

(b)

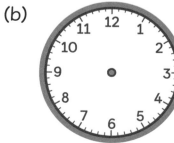

9:45

Telling and writing the time

Starter

What time does this clock show?

Example

It is 15 minutes past 8 or 8:15.
The minute hand is a quarter of the way around the clock.

We can also say the time is quarter past 8.

After 15 more minutes, the minute hand is halfway around the clock.

It is half past 8.

Now the minute hand is three quarters of the way around the clock. It has a quarter turn until it reaches 12 again.

We say the time is 8:45 or quarter to 9.

1 Fill in the blanks using **quarter past, half past** or **quarter to.**

(a)

The time is

[ ] 3.

(b)

The time is

[ ] 10.

(c)

The time is

[ ] 12.

2 Draw the missing hour and minute hands on the clocks to show:

(a) 1 o'clock

(b) quarter past 4

(c) half past 10

(d) quarter to 5

Finding durations of time

Starter

Lulu started reading at 3:30 and finished at 4:00.
For how long did she read?

start

end

Example

Count in fives from 3:30 to 4:00.

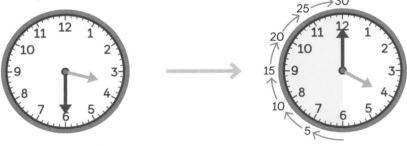

5, 10, 15, 20, 25, 30

Lulu read for 30 minutes.

Practice

1 Write the time shown on each clock. Draw the missing hour and minute hands on the clocks to show the new time.

(a)

30 minutes later

(b)

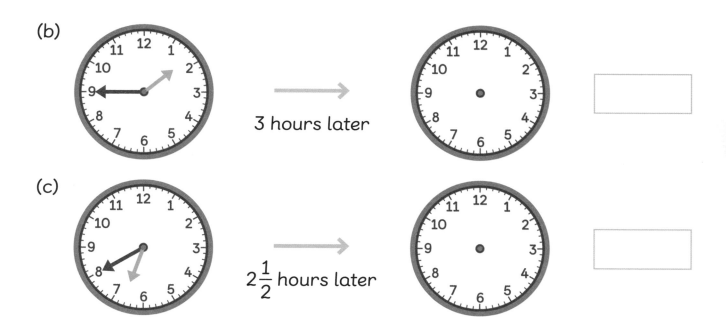

3 hours later

(c)

$2\frac{1}{2}$ hours later

2 Complete the table.

Start time	What time will it be in half an hour?	What time will it be in 2 hours?

Finding ending times

Starter

School assembly starts in 15 minutes.
The assembly lasts for 35 minutes.
At what time does assembly end?

Example

In 15 minutes, the time will be 9:00.

This is the time assembly starts.

School assembly lasts for 35 minutes.

35 minutes later

Assembly finishes at 9:35.

Write the time shown on each clock. Draw the missing hour and minute hands on the clocks to show the new time.

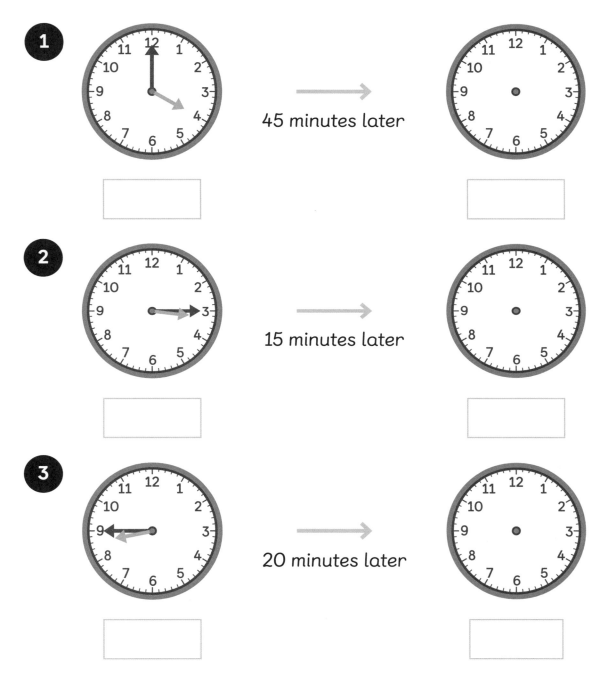

1

45 minutes later

2

15 minutes later

3

20 minutes later

Finding starting times

Starter

Lulu has been swimming for 30 minutes.
The time now is:

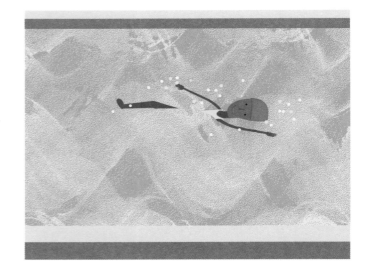

At what time did Lulu start swimming?

Example

What was the time 30 minutes ago?

4 o'clock
half past 4
5 o'clock

It was half past 4.
Lulu started swimming at 4:30.

36

1 Draw the clock hands to show the start times.

(a)

30 minutes later

(b)

15 minutes later

(c)

1 hour later

(d)

45 minutes later

2 A TV programme ended at 6:30. The programme was an hour long. At what time did the programme start?

The TV programme started at  .

Measuring volume in litres

Starter

How can we find the volume of liquid in each container?

Example

We can measure volume using a 1-litre beaker.

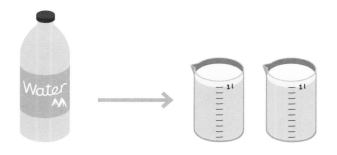

The volume of water is about 2 **litres**.
We can write this as 2 l.

> **Volume** is the amount of liquid in a container.

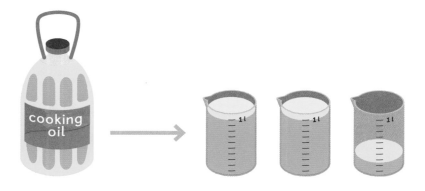

The volume of cooking oil is more than 2 litres.

1 Find some containers with liquid in your kitchen.
Guess the volume of liquid in each container and then
measure the actual volume using a measuring jug.
Record your results in a table.

Item	Guessed volume (in l)	Measured volume (in l)

2 What is the volume of liquid in each container?

(a)

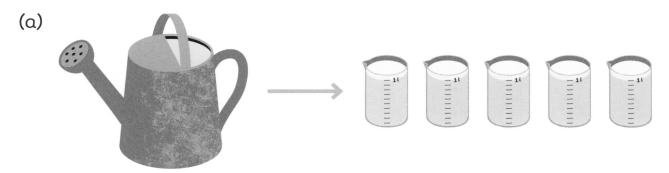

The volume of water in the watering can is [ ] l.

(b)

The volume of chocolate milk in the carton is [ ] l.

Measuring volume in millilitres

Starter

How can we measure smaller volumes of liquid?

Example

We can measure smaller volumes of liquid in millilitres. We write this as ml.

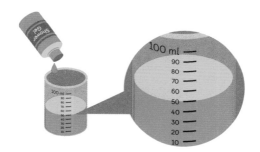

Volume of shower gel = 50 ml

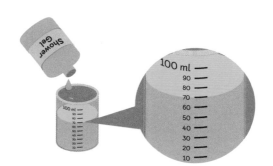

Volume of shower gel = 70 ml

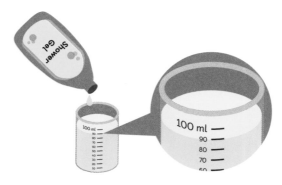

Volume of shower gel = 90 ml

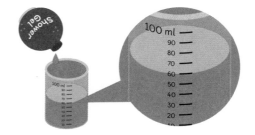

Volume of shower gel = 60 ml

The contains the least volume of shower gel. The contains the greatest volume of shower gel.

40

Fill in the blanks.

1 The volume of water in cup A is [   ] ml.

2 The volume of water in cup C is [   ] ml.

3 The volume of water in cup A is less than the volume of water in cup [   ].

4 The volume of water in cup B is more than the volume of water in cup [   ].

5 Cup [   ] has the greatest volume of water.

6 Cup [   ] has the smallest volume of water.

Review and challenge

1 Find the length of each item.

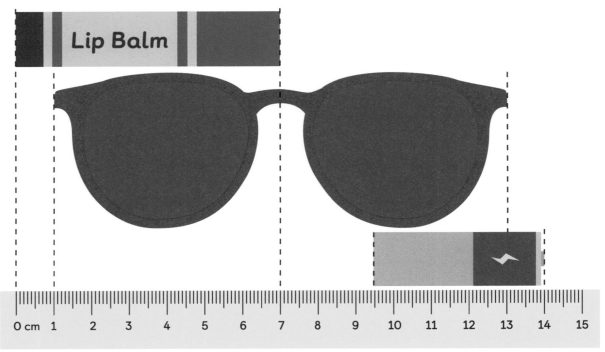

(a) The lip balm is ⬚ cm long.

(b) The sunglasses are ⬚ cm long.

(c) The battery is ⬚ cm long.

(d) The ⬚ is shorter than the lip balm.

2 What is the mass of the mango?

⬚ g

3 The temperature in the fridge is 4 °C.
The temperature in the kitchen is
18 °C warmer.
What is the temperature in the
kitchen?

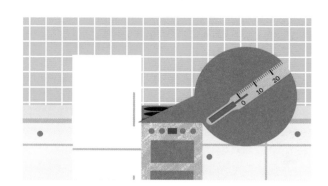

☐ °C

4 Draw different coins to show the same value as the coins below.

(a)

(b)

(c)

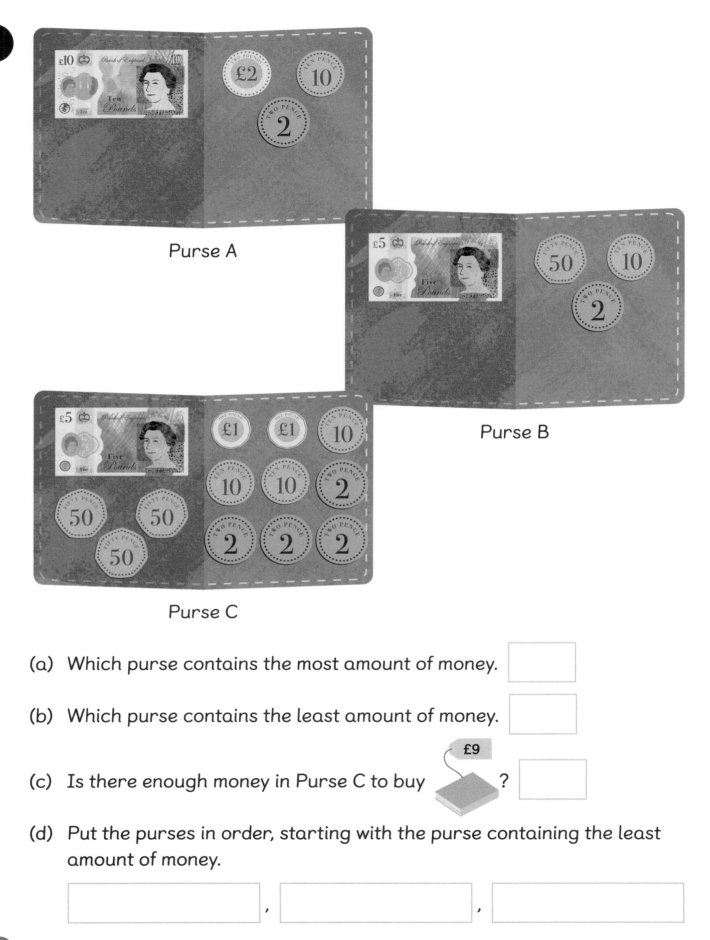

Purse A

Purse B

Purse C

(a) Which purse contains the most amount of money.

(b) Which purse contains the least amount of money.

(c) Is there enough money in Purse C to buy £9 ?

(d) Put the purses in order, starting with the purse containing the least amount of money.

_____ , _____ , _____

6 The clocks show the time Ruby starts each activity.

watches TV   goes to bed   plays football

(a) [ ] is the time that Ruby starts to watch TV.

(b) Ruby starts playing football at [ ].

(c) The last activity of the day is at [ ], when Ruby goes to bed.

(d) Put the activities in order from earliest to latest start time.

[ ] , [ ] , [ ]

7 What is the volume of water in each container?

(a)

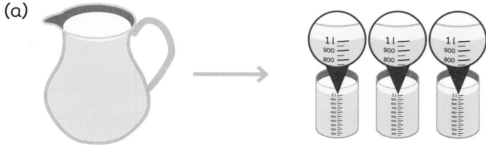

The volume of water in the jug is [ ] l.

(b)

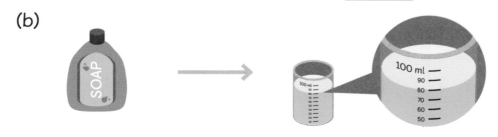

The volume of soap in the bottle is [ ] ml.

45

Answers

Page 5   **3** Answers will vary.

Page 7   **2 (a)** 4 cm **(b)** 7 cm.

Page 9   **1** The lolly stick is 13 cm long. **2** The peg is 8 cm long. **3** The toothbrush is 14 cm long. **4** The toothbrush is 1 cm longer than the lolly stick. **5** The peg is 5 cm shorter than the lolly stick. **6** The toothbrush is the longest. **7** The peg is the shortest.

Page 11   **2** The mass of the watermelon is about 3 kg. **3 (a)** 3 kg **(b)** 8 kg.

Page 13   **2 (a)** 50 g **(b)** 100 g **(c)** 70 g **(d)** 75 g
                3 (a) The sandwich weighs about 100g. **(b)** The mass of the blueberries is about 65 g.

Page 15   **1 (a)** The phone is lighter than the pencil case. **(b)** The mass of the phone is 200 g. **(c)** The mass of the pencil case is 260 g. **(d)** The mass of the phone is 60 g lighter than the mass of the pencil case.
                2 (a) The mass of the orange is 100 g more than the mass of the peach. **(b)** The cherries have the lightest mass. **(c)** The lemon and the peach together have the same mass as the orange.

Page 17   **2 (a)** 20 °C **(b)** 90 °C **(c)** 0 °C.

Page 19   **1 (a)** £15 **(b)** £25 **(c)** £55 **(d)** £55   **2** Amira has £40. Sam has £50. Sam has more money.

Page 21   **1**

                2 (a) 88p **(b)** £5 and 55p

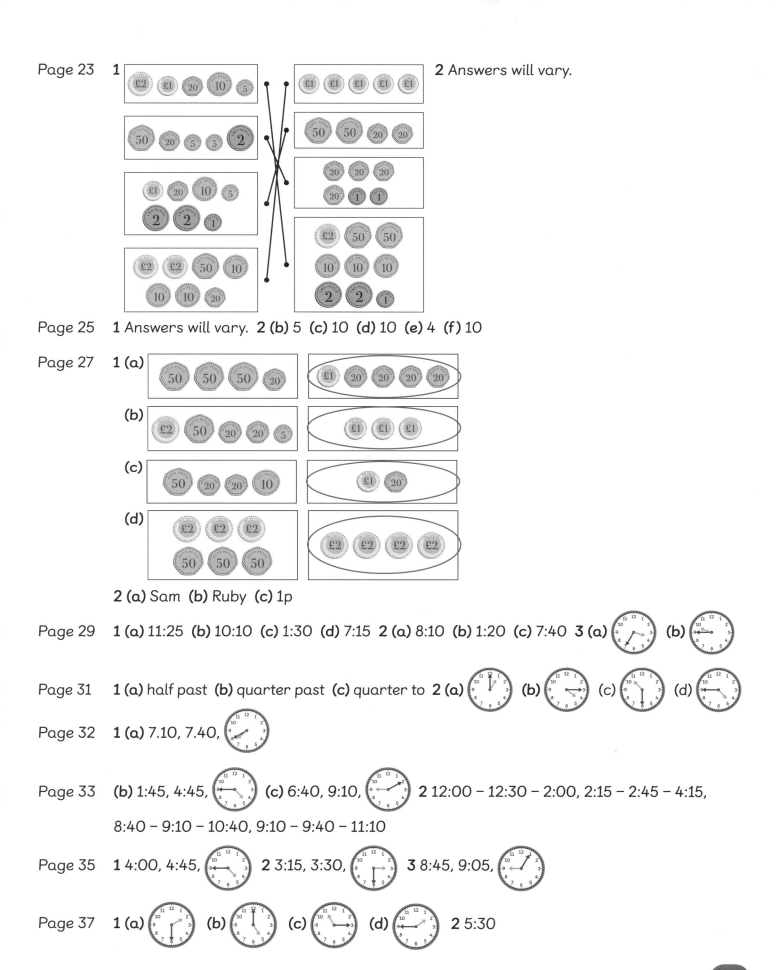

Page 23   **1**   **2** Answers will vary.

Page 25   **1** Answers will vary.   **2 (b)** 5 **(c)** 10 **(d)** 10 **(e)** 4 **(f)** 10

Page 27   **1 (a)**

       (b)

       (c)

       (d)

   2 (a) Sam **(b)** Ruby **(c)** 1p

Page 29   **1 (a)** 11:25 **(b)** 10:10 **(c)** 1:30 **(d)** 7:15 **2 (a)** 8:10 **(b)** 1:20 **(c)** 7:40 **3 (a)**   **(b)**

Page 31   **1 (a)** half past **(b)** quarter past **(c)** quarter to **2 (a)** **(b)** **(c)** **(d)**

Page 32   **1 (a)** 7.10, 7.40,

Page 33   **(b)** 1:45, 4:45, **(c)** 6:40, 9:10, **2** 12:00 – 12:30 – 2:00, 2:15 – 2:45 – 4:15, 8:40 – 9:10 – 10:40, 9:10 – 9:40 – 11:10

Page 35   **1** 4:00, 4:45, **2** 3:15, 3:30, **3** 8:45, 9:05,

Page 37   **1 (a)** **(b)** **(c)** **(d)** **2** 5:30

47

Answers continued

Page 39   **2 (a)** 5 l   **(b)** 1 l

Page 41   **1** The volume of water in cup A is 60 ml.   **2** The volume of water in cup C is 90 ml.
     3 The volume of water in cup A is less than the volume of water in cup C.
     4 The volume of water in cup B is more than the volume of water in cup D.
     5 Cup C has the greatest volume of water.   **6** Cup D has the smallest volume of water.

Page 42   **1 (a)** The lip balm is 7 cm long.   **(b)** The sunglasses are 12 cm long.
     (c) The battery is 4.5 cm long.   **(d)** The battery is shorter than the lip balm.   **2** 200 g

Page 43   **3** 22 °C   **4 (a–c)** Answers will vary.

Page 44   **5 (a)** Purse A   **(b)** Purse B   **(c)** no   **(d)** Purse B, Purse C, Purse A.

Page 45   **6 (a)** 6:15 is the time that Ruby starts to watch TV.   **(b)** Ruby starts playing football at 4:45.
     (c) The last activity of the day is at 8:30, when Ruby goes to bed.   **(d)** plays football,
     watches TV, goes to bed   **7 (a)** The volume of water in the jug is 3 l.   **(b)** The volume of soap
     in the bottle is 80 ml.